The Power of the BR Standard 4-6-0s

Of the 172 Standard '5MTs', the Scottish Region was allocated 51 new members
of the class, although five (Nos 73032-6) stayed for less than two months.
No 73077, which spent 7½ years at Eastfield, is seen piloting Thompson 'B1'
4-6-0 No 61396 (also from Eastfield) at the head of the 10.15am Glasgow
Queen Street–Fort William on 13 August 1960. The train is approaching
Tyndrum Upper. *Gavin Morrison*

No 73163 prepares to leave Leeds City on a train for Llandudno on 19 June 1965. By this time it was three months away from withdrawal, and in terrible external condition — not uncommon for members of the class allocated to Patricroft shed in the last years of steam. It went new to York shed in February 1957 and stayed in the North Eastern Region, mainly at Huddersfield, for nearly six years before moving to Wolverhampton Oxley and ultimately Patricroft. *Gavin Morrison*

1M71

The Power of the BR Standard 4-6-0s

Gavin Morrison

An imprint of
Ian Allan Publishing

Contents

Introduction

First published 2003

ISBN 0 86093 577 9

Published by Ian Allan Publishing

an imprint of Ian Allan Publishing Ltd, Hersham, Surrey KT12 4RG.
Printed by Ian Allan Printing Ltd, Hersham, Surrey KT12 4RG.

Code: 0306/B

Waiting for a train at Carlisle recently, I noticed the well-painted works plate of a Fragonset Class 31 diesel, indicating construction at Brush in 1959, some 43 years ago, and was struck by the contrast in longevity between the last remaining early BR diesels and the BR Standard '5MT' and '4MT' 4-6-0s, which managed an average of just 15 years in service.

By most accounts the Standard '5MTs' were fine engines, but, looking back, it is unclear why these 172 locomotives were ever built; with the exception of the Southern-allocated members and the few that went to the Somerset & Dorset line, they were used not to replace older locomotives but rather to augment the existing Stanier Class 5s or Great Western 'Halls' and 'Granges', whereas the 80 Standard '4MT' 4-6-0s replaced many ageing 4-4-0s and 0-6-0s which could not have been retained economically until the end of steam and were thus generally better appreciated by crews.

As might be expected with such a short time in service, there were very few alterations to the classes after building. The Standard '5MTs' remained basically unaltered, whilst a few '4MT' 4-6-0s received double chimneys, which according to Southern footplate crews improved their performance. In the author's view both were handsome designs, although their appearance was affected greatly by the type of tender attached: the '5MTs' suited various tenders, but the high-water-capacity BR1B tenders attached to '4MT' locomotives allocated originally to the Southern Region always seemed just a little too big. BR lined black livery was standard for all locomotives when new, but in 1956 the Western Region decided to paint its examples in lined Brunswick green.

The Standard '5MTs' could be found anywhere between Inverness, Holyhead, Plymouth and Margate; the only areas where they were not around in any great numbers were the Eastern and North Eastern Regions, where, in addition to 410 'B1s' and 184 'V2s', there were so many Pacifics that these could be found on local three- or four-coach stopping trains. Similarly, these two Regions (in common with Scotland) never received any of the '4MT' 4-6-0s.

Title page:
Class 4MT 4-6-0 No 75061 was one of a batch of 15 such locomotives with Type 2A tenders, all allocated to the London Midland Region. It is seen at Derby on 27 April 1963. *R. A. Panting*

Both classes were initially allocated in small numbers to a wide variety of sheds. As might be expected, the Western Region didn't take to them, while the LMR sheds seemed to like or dislike them, according to how many Stanier Class 5s were already allocated, or whether or not they were replacing LMS Compounds, '2P' 4-4-0s or 0-6-0s.

Unlike the 'Britannia' Pacifics and (to a lesser degree) the '9F' 2-10-0s, which are remembered for particular workings, the '5MTs' really made a name for themselves in only a few places. Chief among these was the Somerset & Dorset line, where a few took over the main express workings in 1954, and where the '4MT' 4-6-0s also had a long association. The North Wales Coast was another area where both classes were well represented, while the 10 Caprotti '5MTs' allocated to Glasgow Balornock turned in consistently fine performances on Glasgow–Dundee expresses for a period of around eight years.

The '5MTs' were well represented on the Midland main line and the Bristol route but in the early years seldom appeared often over Shap on the West Coast main line. The '4MT' 4-6-0s were allocated to Bletchley for commuter services into Euston.

The Scottish Region received a large number of Standard '5MTs', whereas no '4MT' 4-6-0s were ever allocated. When new, Nos 73005-9 at Perth were used on the Glasgow Buchanan Street–Aberdeen expresses such as the 'Saint Mungo' and the 'Granite City', Nos 73077/8 from Eastfield put in a few years' work on the West Highland line and Nos 73105-9 shared Glasgow Queen Street–Edinburgh Waverley workings with Haymarket's various Pacifics and 'B1' 4-6-0s. While the Corkerhill locomotives became the main power on the Glasgow–Stranraer workings, the Polmadie engines covered a wide variety of jobs.

Apart from the Somerset & Dorset and (prior to electrification) Kent Coast workings the '5MTs' could be found on any workings. By contrast the '4MTs', with their wide route availability, could be seen almost everywhere south of the border except for the Eastern and North Eastern Regions, and it was not until the London Midland Region took over the Cambrian lines that they became identified with a particular area, although (as already mentioned) they had long association with the Somerset & Dorset and certain Southern Region services.

Gradually, as diesels took over, the Standard '5MT' and '4MT' 4-6-0s were ousted from certain areas; being the

newest and, in the case of the '4MTs', extremely versatile locomotives, they were retained in preference to older classes. Sheds such as Patricroft received large numbers of '5MTs' — far more than were needed — whilst the Southern Region received additional examples from other Regions. The Cambrian lines were eventually monopolised by the '4MT' 4-6-0s, and sheds such as Stoke received many members of the class. The '4MTs' will also be remembered by enthusiasts for their banking duties on Shap (until the end of 1967) and for the part they took in the last steam workings on BR, hauling ballast trains from Rylstone Quarry to Skipton and pick-up goods from Carnforth. Both classes survived to the last month of BR steam, No 73069 being the last Standard '5MT', while five '4MTs' lasted right to the end.

Fortunately both classes are well represented in preservation, there being five '5MTs' — Nos 73050, 73082, 73096, 73129 and 73156 — although No 73096 is the only one thus far to have worked on the main line; in the case of the '4MTs' there are six preserved — Nos 75014, 75027, 75029, 75069, 75078, 75079 — of which Nos 75014 and 75069 have been used on the main line (although No 75029 attended the S&D150 celebrations in 1979). It is worth mentioning that, since it was saved from Barry scrapyard, No 75078 has put in 30 years' work on the Keighley & Worth Valley Railway, compared to the 10 years it completed for British Railways.

At the time of writing No 73129 — the only Caprotti '5MT' in preservation — is nearing the end of a lengthy

Above:
The branch from Skipton to Grassington was home to one of the last regular steam freight workings on British Rail. Standard '4MTs' Nos 75019 (in lined black livery) and 75027 (in lined green) were regular performers and were kept well cleaned by local enthusiasts. Here No 75019, with a loaded ballast train, puts on a special display of smoke for the photographer as it slows for the crew to open the level-crossing gates at Rylston on 1 June 1968.
Gavin Morrison

restoration and should soon return to the main line; hopefully this will provide the opportunity to compare the performances of standard and Caprotti '5MTs', which was never really done in BR days.

Gavin Morrison
May 2003

Author's note
This book in the 'Power' series has been compiled in an attempt to show all the variations in the BR Standard '4MT' and '5MT' 4-6-0 classes and to illustrate the areas in which they could be found at work. Details of dates and allocations have been obtained largely from the excellent publication *The Book of the BR Standards*, written by Richard Derry and published by Irwell Press, which also contains technical details of these locomotives.

Class 5MT

A superbly atmospheric shot of No 73075 leaving Glasgow Central with a rush-hour train on 23 July 1964. Polmadie was obviously very short of cleaners in the mid-1960s. No 73075 had been new to the shed in April 1955 and would stay until withdrawn in December 1965. *P. Riley*

Variations

Above left:
A general view of a BR Standard Class 5MT under construction, before wheeling. *Ian Allan Library*

Above right:
A tender tank before mounting on the frame for one of the early batch of Standard '5MTs'. *Ian Allan Library*

Left:
An official picture of No 73000 as it emerged from Derby Works in April 1951, having cost £17,603. It is attached to a BR Type 1 tender, with capacity for 4,250 gallons of water and 7 tons of coal. Note the three-tone chime whistle behind the chimney; from No 73100 this was relocated in front of the cab, and in later years earlier members of the class were modified in this way. Note also the fluted coupling rods; from No 73050 these were rectangular in section. *Ian Allan Library*

Lower left:
Nos 73030 and 73031were fitted with Westinghouse air pumps similar to those attached to 'Britannias' Nos 70043 and 70044. These were for trials with an air-braked coal train, conducted at the southern end of the Midland main line in October 1952. The compressor attached to the smokebox is clearly visible in this picture, taken at Derby on 19 June 1953; the air reservoir was under the running-plate in front of the cab. The locomotives returned to standard condition after the trials. *R. J. Buckley*

Above:
From October 1956 locomotives overhauled at Swindon emerged in lined green livery, although it is hard to tell from this picture of No 73035 at Holbeck shed on 17 April 1967. Note that the whistle has been moved to in front of the cab. This locomotive was new to Polmadie in August 1953 but was transferred the following month to Shrewsbury and stayed on the Western Region until transferred in July 1965 to Patricroft, where it ended its days in January 1968. *Gavin Morrison*

Below:
Scottish Region locomotives repaired at St Rollox Works received larger-than-normal cabside numbers. Seen on St Rollox shed (also known as Balornock) on 27 March 1964, No 73056 would spend 10 years at Polmadie before ending its career with an 11-month spell at Aberdeen Ferryhill. Although not apparent from this picture, it is attached to a BR Type 1H tender, which varied from the Type 1 in being fitted with a fall plate and gangway doors. Nos 73053-64 were the only Standard '5MTs' with this type of tender. *Gavin Morrison*

Left:
Only three members of the class
(Nos 73050-2) were attached to the
Type 1G tender when new. Externally
there was little difference from Types 1
and 1H, but the water capacity was
increased to 5,000 gallons, and again
there was 7 tons' coal capacity, which
seems to be at its maximum in this
picture of No 73051! The locomotive
is piloting rebuilt 'West Country'
No 34046 *Braunton* on the
southbound 'Pines Express', seen on
the 1-in-50 climb out of Bath to the
summit at the entrance to Coombe
Down Tunnel on 23 April 1962. Both
firemen have made sure there is little
exhaust before entering the preceding
single-bore Devonshire Tunnel.
Gavin Morrison

Above:
Caprotti locomotives (Nos 73125-54) aside, there was little
variation in the appearance of the class, but attaching
higher-capacity tenders did alter the overall appearance
considerably. The Type 1C tender could carry 9 tons of coal
and 4,725 gallons of water, and was attached to many
locomotives, starting with No 73065. Here No 73067
simmers gently on Farnley Junction shed, Leeds, on 9 July
1960, during its three-year allocation to Holyhead shed
(6J). New in October 1954, it survived until March 1968,
ending its days at Patricroft. *Gavin Morrison*

Left:
Nos 73080-9 were new to Stewarts Lane shed (73A) in South London between June and September 1955. As there were no water troughs on the Southern Region they received Type 1B tenders with capacity for 7 tons of coal and 4,725 gallons of water. In March 1957, before it was named *Joyous Gard* (previously carried by Southern 'King Arthur' No 30741), No 73088 stands on Derby shed, no doubt after a visit to the adjacent works. *Gavin Morrison*

Right:
Yet another tender variation was the Type 1F attached to Nos 73110-9, all of which went new to Nine Elms shed (70A) between October and December 1955. These tenders had the highest water capacity — 5,625 gallons — of all the BR Standard tenders and were attached to many of the Class 9F 2-10-0s. '5MT' No 73116, seen at Eastleigh shed, was named *Iseult* (the plate being visible above the centre driving wheel), formerly carried by 'King Arthur' No 30739. *Ian Allan Library*

Right:
A picture clearly showing the Caprotti valve gear on No 73126, taken at Eastleigh on 12 February 1965 after a works visit. This locomotive was only ever allocated to Shrewsbury and Patricroft, spending almost 10 years at the latter before being withdrawn in April 1968. *G. H. Wheeler*

The Caprottis

Upper left:
Thirty members of the class — Nos 73125-54 — were delivered from Derby Works in 1956 fitted with British Caprotti valve gear, due (it is said) to the good results obtained with No 71000 *Duke of Gloucester* and the batch of ex-LMS Class 5MTs. This is an official picture of the first example No 73125 as it emerged from Derby Works in July 1956 attached to a BR Type 1B tender. It was decided to allocate 10 each to the Western, London Midland and Scottish Regions, which now seems a strange decision as it resulted in no area really becoming expert as far as maintenance and driving were concerned, although the Scottish examples — all allocated to St Rollox — nevertheless put in some fast performances on the Glasgow Buchanan Street–Dundee trains. The Western and Midland examples nearly all eventually ended up at Patricroft. Whether the Caprottis were better performers than the standard locomotives was never really established; maybe when the preserved No 73129 returns to the main line, it will be possible to draw comparisons with the other preserved examples. *Ian Allan Library*

Centre left:
A close-up of the Caprotti valve gear of No 73144, taken at Cricklewood shed on 29 April 1961. *F. J. Saunders*

Lower left:
A rear view of No 73129 a month after it arrived new at Shrewsbury shed in August 1956. This became the only Caprotti Standard '5MT' to be preserved and is currently under restoration at Butterley. *P. J. Kelley*

Above:
With the help of a banker, Patricroft's No 73141 makes a spectacular departure from Bradford Exchange up the 1-in-50 climb to Bowling Junction on 1 July 1967. The train was the Summer Saturdays-only to Bridlington, by this time the longest steam diagram in the area, and the Low Moor crews put up some high-speed runs on the stretch between Selby and Hull. The Type 1C tender seems to have its full 9 tons of coal on board. *Gavin Morrison*

Below:
It was quite unusual to see a Caprotti Standard '5MT' heading north out of Leeds, but on 17 September 1963 Carnforth shed had borrowed Patricroft's No 73132 to work the 1.54pm from Leeds City to Carnforth. The picture was taken from the signalbox at Wortley Junction and shows the bridge in the background carrying the old Great Northern main line into Leeds Central. The number of tracks at this location is now reduced to four. *Gavin Morrison*

Left:
An immaculate No 73130 waits on the ash pits at York shed before returning to its home base of Patricroft on 6 February 1964. By this time its 26F shedplate should have been replaced by 9H, following the reclassification of sheds in the Manchester area in September 1963.
Gavin Morrison

Left:
Another Patricroft Caprotti freshly ex works at Darlington shed on 10 October 1964, carrying the new 9H shedplate. Note the piece of string from the handrail (supporting a lubricator) and that there is no lining on the running-plate. This pictures clearly show also the pipes normally hidden under the running-plate of the Standard locomotives. Another variation is the gap in the running-plate above the rear driving wheel, to accommodate the lubricators which were driven off the rear driving wheel.
Gavin Morrison

Left:
A fine study of St Rollox-allocated No 73150 at its home shed on 17 May 1964. Built April 1957, this locomotive would spend almost its entire career at St Rollox, moving to Stirling only a month before withdrawal in December 1966.
P. H. Groom

Above:
No 73153 descends the 1-in-79 gradient from Milton Junction to Glasgow Buchanan Street at the head of the 10.00am Dundee express on 19 January 1963. The manual coaling stage of St Rollox shed is clearly visible in this picture. The lines on the right went to St Rollox Works. No 73153 was another member of the St Rollox batch of 10 to spend all but one month of its career at the shed, being withdrawn from Stirling in December 1966. *S. Richard*

Right:
Hauling one of the many end-of-steam specials around Lancashire and Yorkshire, No 73134, one of the last operational Caprotti members of the class, pilots No 73069, which would become the last Standard 5MT in service, past Spring Valley on the Blackburn–Bolton line. An attempt has been made to clean the leading locomotive, but there is little sign of the lining or badge on the tender. It would be withdrawn in June 1968, two months after this picture was taken on 20 April 1968.
Gavin Morrison

Above:
No 73171 was the last member of the class to be built, in May 1957, and was allocated to York. Seen at Leeds Holbeck shed on 12 October 1961, it would stay on the North Eastern Region until sent to Feltham in September 1963, thereafter remaining on the Southern Region until withdrawn in October 1966 after just over nine years of service. *Gavin Morrison*

On shed

Left:
No 73069 stands on Holbeck shed, where it was allocated for four years from 1955 to 1959, but when this picture was taken on 10 September 1963 the locomotive was based at Cricklewood. It would become one of the last of its class in service, being withdrawn from Carnforth shed at the end of BR steam. *Gavin Morrison*

Above:
Twenty members of the class — Nos 73080-9 and
73110-9, all based on the Southern Region — received
names formerly carried by the famous 'King Arthur' class
locomotives. *Lyonnesse* was carried by No 73113 and
originally by 'King Arthur' No 30743. *D. A. Davies*

Above:
No 73089 received the name *Maid of Astolat* previously
carried by 'King Arthur' No 30744. *J. C. Haydon*

Above:
No 73110 *The Red Knight* stands on Eastleigh shed on 29 August 1961.
Gavin Morrison

Left:
Brand-new No 73001 presents a fine sight in BR lined black livery outside Derby shed in May 1951. *J. Larkin*

Right:
In addition to its regular Somerset & Dorset Standard '5MTs', Bath Green Park used to have the loan of one or two of the Southern Region examples during the summer months. No 73087 *Linette* was on loan during the 1961 summer timetable and is seen about to leave the shed with ex-LMS '2P' 4-4-0 No 40700 to take over the Saturdays-only Birmingham New Street–Bournemouth on 9 September 1961.
Gavin Morrison

Left:
Surrounded by ex-Great Western locomotives, No 73019 stands at Cardiff East Dock shed when allocated to Gloucester Barnwood. Allocated to Nottingham when new in October 1951, it moved to Bristol St Philip's Marsh shed in September 1953 and would stay on the Western Region for most of its life, until transferred in April 1966 to Bolton, being withdrawn in January 1967.
G. T. Storer

Right:
A fine atmospheric picture of a run-down Caprotti member of the class, at Patricroft shed on 8 June 1967. No 73140 shows off its dirty front with painted 9H shed code. This locomotive was new to Leicester Midland in December 1956 and, except for a 17-month spell at Holyhead, spent most of its days working from LMR sheds in and around Derby, before being withdrawn in October 1967.
J. A. M. Vaughan

Below:
Sunday morning at Stranraer shed (68C): nothing stirs on 2 July 1961 as Corkerhill-based '5MT' No 73100 stands alongside No 76112, then the only locally-allocated Standard '4MT' 2-6-0. On the right is Dumfries-allocated Hughes 'Crab' 2-6-0 No 42919. *Gavin Morrison*

Left:
No73009 was one of the early batch of five Class 5MTs (Nos 73005-9) allocated to Perth (63A) when new, primarily for working the Aberdeen–Glasgow Buchanan Street expresses, as well as trains over the Highland lines to Inverness. It is seen at Glasgow St Rollox (Balornock) shed (code 65B) on 25 August 1962, by which time its duties on such trains had been taken over by Gresley Pacifics. It stayed at Perth from July 1951 to January 1963 and then moved to Corkerhill shed, from where it was withdrawn in July 1966.
Gavin Morrison

Above:
Another picture taken at St Rollox (Balornock), this time showing No 73148, one of the 10 Caprotti locomotives allocated new to the shed in the first six months of 1957, on the ash pits. Visible in the background is the manual coaling stage; the shed was at a higher level to the left of the picture. The locomotive was withdrawn in September 1965 after 8½ years' service at the shed. *Gavin Morrison*

Right:
The day's work is over for the driver and fireman of Patricroft-based No 73157 on 12 September 1957.
J. A. M. Vaughan

Above:
A fine atmospheric picture taken at Patricroft shed on 20 December 1965, showing two Standard '5MTs'. *L. A. Nixon*

Left:
Another picture on Patricroft shed, showing the appalling condition of some of its allocation of Standard '5MTs' during the last few months of steam on BR. Caprotti No 73126 was new to Shrewsbury in July 1956, transferring in August 1958 to Patricroft, where it remained until withdrawn in April 1968, the month after this picture was taken on 27 March 1968. *K. P. Lawrence*

Left:
When brand-new in August 1956, No 73129 awaits a running-in turn at Derby shed before starting its working days at Shrewsbury, where it would stay for two years before moving to Patricroft in August 1958. After withdrawal in November 1967 it ended up at Barry scrapyard, from where it became the 32nd locomotive to be rescued for preservation, in January 1973, and the only Caprotti member of the class to be saved. It is still under restoration, some 35 years after withdrawal. *R. J. Buckley*

Left:
No 73071 on the ash pits at York shed, prior to returning to its home shed of Woodford Halse (1G) after an overhaul at Darlington Works on 29 May 1964. This locomotive was one of the few members of the class to be allocated to the Eastern Region, being based at King's Cross shed between February 1956 and March 1957. It was allocated to a wide variety of sheds but, like many others, finished at Patricroft, being withdrawn in September 1967. *Gavin Morrison*

Right:
Prior to being named *Linette*, No 73087 is watered at Stewarts Lane (73A) before heading off shed to take up a working from Victoria station. One of the batch of 10 (Nos 73080-9) allocated new to this shed in 1955, it was eventually withdrawn from Guildford in October 1966. *A. R. Carpenter*

Above:
New to Patricroft shed in October 1955, No 73092 spent time on the London Midland, Western and Southern Regions, finishing its days at Guildford in July 1967.

During this final phase of its career, on 26 March 1967, it is seen at Bournemouth shed alongside rebuilt 'Merchant Navy' No 35013 *Blue Funnel.* Cabside apart, there is little evidence that it is painted green. *Gavin Morrison*

Above:
The last of the class to be built in May 1957 was No 73171, seen receiving attention at Nine Elms (70A) on 4 July 1966, three months before withdrawal. It ended its days allocated to Eastleigh shed (71A), after barely nine years of service. *M. S. Stokes*

Above:
The end of steam on the Southern Region came on 9 July 1967. Seen at the back of Basingstoke shed, No 73093 has been decorated (if that is the correct term) by the staff for its last journey in steam to Salisbury, where it would be formally withdrawn. *K. P. Lawrence*

Left:
A fine illustration of Southern Region steam depicts Standard '5MT' No 73080 (before being named *Merlin*) in the company of 'Schools' class 4-4-0 No 30929 *Malvern* and unrebuilt 'Battle of Britain' No 34084 *253 Squadron* at the head of a boat train. The picture was taken looking east at Folkestone Junction on 19 July 1958. *S. Creer*

Below:
While allocated to Woodford Halse on the ex-Great Central line, No 73032 headed the Summer Saturdays-only Eastbourne–Walsall train up the Quarry Line at Earlswood on 25 July 1964. The locomotive led a somewhat nomadic existence, being allocated to the Scottish, Western and London Midland Regions before being withdrawn from Croes Newydd in August 1965.
G. D. King

Right:
The Standard '5MTs' at Stewarts Lane were very well liked by the crews. In July 1956, when just under a year old, No 73087 (later named *Linette*) is seen at an unidentified location whilst working a Kent Coast express. *Ian Allan Library*

Below:
A fine picture of the 'Southern Wanderer' railtour, headed by a well-groomed No 73022, taken between Horsham and Pulborough on 28 March 1965. The locomotive was then allocated to Eastleigh but would end its days at Nine Elms, in April 1967. *D. Hill*

Above:
The minimum of cleaning has been done on Nine Elms' No 73110 as it prepares to leave Waterloo on the 5.39pm to Salisbury in August 1958. Note the large numbers. *Brian Morrison*

Left:
No 73119 *Elaine* heads the 11.30am Waterloo–
Bournemouth West, consisting of 11 coaches and one
van, past Clapham Junction on 30 August 1964. After
nearly nine years allocated to Nine Elms from new it was
transferred during August 1964 to Eastleigh, where it
would remain until withdrawn in March 1967.
Brian Stephenson

Above:
A superb, panned action shot of No 73022, still with its
whistle behind the chimney, as it speeds east through
Basingstoke with an express from Weymouth on
5 September 1964. The locomotive would last almost
until the end of steam on the Southern Region, being
withdrawn only in April 1967. *Paul Riley*

Right:
No 73022 prepares to leave Basingstoke on a down
express on 24 September 1966 while allocated to Nine
Elms, from which shed it would be withdrawn in April
1967. *Gavin Morrison*

Left:
A fine picture of No 73087, later named *Linette*, pulling away from Eastleigh with a Wolverhampton–Portsmouth excursion on 26 September 1956. The locomotive still carried a Stewarts Lane shedplate (73A) but had been allocated to Bath Green Park since August and would move to Eastleigh in October. *L. Elsey*

Right:
Although transferred to Nine Elms from Stewarts Lane some 3¼ years previously, No 73083 *Pendragon* had still not had its shedplate altered from 73A to 70A when it was photographed passing through Eastleigh station with a Waterloo–Bournemouth express on 4 August 1962. It would be withdrawn from Weymouth shed in September 1966. *Gavin Morrison*

Left:
Eastleigh-allocated No 73111, formerly named *King Uther*, heads across Brockenhurst Common with a down express on 9 September 1965; it would be withdrawn the following month. Of its brief (10-year) career, nearly nine years were spent at Nine Elms. *Gavin Morrison*

Above:
After almost nine years at Nine Elms, where it was allocated from new, No 73111 was transferred to Eastleigh in August 1964. It is pictured on 12 September 1964 heading a Waterloo–Bournemouth express under the fine gantry which once graced the west end of Southampton Central station. The locomotive would survive until October 1965. *Gavin Morrison*

Right:
Seen pulling away from Christchurch without a trace of exhaust on a hot summer Saturday (9 June 1962), No 73116 seems to have lost its *Iseult* nameplates. It would be the first of the original 20 locomotives allocated to the Southern Region to be withdrawn — in November 1964, after only nine years' service. *Gavin Morrison*

Left:
No 73029 shows little of its green paintwork as it prepares to leave Bournemouth Central with an express for Waterloo on 22 July 1966. New to Blackpool in January 1952, this locomotive subsequently moved to the Western Region, where it stayed until transferred to Weymouth in September 1958. It would stay on the Southern Region until withdrawn in July 1967, latterly being one of the last of the class on the Southern and used on some of the last Southern steam specials. *Gavin Morrison*

Below
A filthy No 73118, once named *King Leodegrance*, heads an up Waterloo express past Bournemouth West Junction on 1 September 1965. New to Nine Elms in December 1955, it would spend all its days allocated to the Southern Region, being withdrawn from Guildford in October 1966. *Gavin Morrison*

Left:
An atmospheric early-morning picture of two Standard '5MTs' — Nos 73017 and 73020 — tackling the 1-in-74/50 climb from Weymouth to Bincombe Tunnel and Upwey Halt on 1 September 1962. *D. H. Cape*

Right:
No 73087, minus *Linette* nameplates, climbs out of Weymouth with an up boat train on Saturday 30 September 1961. It is receiving banking assistance up to Bincombe 'box from Class 4MT 2-6-0 No 76060. *Gavin Morrison*

Right:
The return leg of the 'Dorset Coast Express' — a special run on 7 May 1967 by the Locomotive Club of Great Britain — prepares to leave Weymouth behind green-liveried Standard '5MT' No 73029, with Standard '4MT' 2-6-0 No 76026 as pilot. This locomotive was one of the last active members of its class on the Southern Region, surviving until July 1967. *Gavin Morrison*

On the Somerset & Dorset

Above:

It is perhaps appropriate to start the section on the S&D with a picture of the first Standard '5MT' to be allocated to Bath Green Park. Along with Nos 73051 and 73052 No 73050 arrived around the end of May or early June 1954, this trio being the first new tender engines allocated to Bath Green Park for many years. No 73050 heads a Bristol– Bournemouth train through the delightful countryside of the Milford Valley in June 1959. This locomotive would eventually move to pastures new, but Nos 73051 and 73052 would remain until withdrawn. *D. Cross*

Right:

No 73054 arrived at Bath Green Park in April 1961 and stayed until withdrawn in August 1965. It is seen at the head of a Bristol–Bournemouth train at Bath Junction as '2MT' 2-6-2T No 41304 approaches the station on 18 July 1963. *D. Cross*

Right:
In the early 1960s Bath Green Park was usually loaned an additional Standard '5MT' from a Southern shed during the summer months. In 1961 this locomotive was No 73087, being seen (without its *Linette* nameplates) on 12 August with a Saturdays-only Birmingham New Street–Bournemouth express and being piloted out of Chilcompton Tunnel, on its way to Masbury Summit, by long-time S&D 4-4-0 No 40700.
Gavin Morrison

Right:
A delightful scene at the country station of Sturminster Newton, as Bath Green Park's No 73052 arrives with the 15.40 from Bournemouth to Bristol on 4 September 1964.
A. Muckley

Right:
A picture — showing the last train on the Limpley Stoke–Camerton line to pass underneath the S&D at Midford — which was doubtless carefully organised for photographer Ivo Peters. 0-6-0PT No 9628 heads a demolition train as Standard '5MT' No 73116 passes with the 11am goods from Bath on 30 June 1958.
Ivo Peters

Left:
The first of two pictures of Somerset & Dorset trains at the southern end of the line, in Southern Region territory. No 73054 seems to be producing an excessive quantity of smoke as it pauses at Broadstone station at the head of a Bath–Bournemouth train in July 1963. *R. Kell*

Left:
No 73001's tender looks nearly empty as it rolls into Parkstone — virtually at the end of its journey from Bath to Bournemouth — on 7 September 1965. As a matter of pride, S&D crews always climbed the steep bank from Poole to Branksome — mainly at 1 in 50/60 — without bankers, whereas the Southern main-line and cross-country trains frequently took them. The condition of the locomotive is in sharp contrast to those already included in the book; its last shed was Bath Green Park, where it had little opportunity to show off its green livery. Withdrawal would come in December 1965. *Gavin Morrison*

Left:
Driver Dick Eury at the controls of No 73047 near Templecombe. *Hugh Ballantyne*

Right:
Swindon's No 73018 leaves Paignton with a Kingswear–Paddington express in 1957. In September 1958 this locomotive was transferred to the Southern, where it would remain until withdrawn from Guildford shed in July 1967. *Ian Allan Library*

On the Western Region

Left:
No 73018 prepares to leave Frome for its then home of Weymouth on 31 July 1965. It had begun its working life on the London Midland Region at Nottingham in October 1951, moving in 1953 to the Western Region and finally to the Southern Region, where it would remain until withdrawn from Guildford in April 1967.
Hugh Ballantyne

Right:
A father gives his son a lift to look into the cab while No 73027 pauses at Chipping Sodbury with a local service from Swindon to Bristol on 25 March 1961. The locomotive was new in December 1951 to Blackpool, staying for just under two years before going to Bristol St Philip's Marsh (for less than a year) and thence in July 1954 to Swindon, where it would remain until withdrawn in February 1964.
Hugh Ballantyne

Above:
On 2 July 1962 a clean, green-liveried No 73036 prepares to leave Swansea Victoria for Shrewsbury, where it was based for 10¾ of its 12 years of service. Swansea Victoria station would close to passengers on 15 June 1964.
Gavin Morrison

Below:
Another Shrewsbury-allocated Standard '5MT' on the Central Wales line, this time No 73026 with the 2.40pm Shrewsbury–Swansea Victoria on 10 August 1963. The fireman is leaning well out of the cab to exchange single-line tablets with the signalman at Sugar Loaf Summit 'box.
G. T. Robinson

Right:
Heading north on the Central Wales line behind Shrewsbury 'Standard' No 73036, a Swansea–Shrewsbury train slows for Derwydd Road 'box to exchange the tablet on 19 May 1964.
Hugh Ballantyne

Left:
A fine shot of the scenic location of Builth Road, taken on 10 June 1964. On the high level is Shrewsbury '5MT' No 73090 with the 11.45 Shrewsbury–Swansea Victoria, whilst on the low level is the track-lifting train at work on the last remaining section of the line between Llanidloes and Three Cocks Junction.
B. J. Ashworth

Right:
Shrewsbury station in October 1963. The 8.55am Birkenhead–Paddington, headed by No 73067 of Chester Midland shed (6A), has just arrived at Platform 4; at Platform 5 is the 7.35 from Aberystwyth. No 73067 would move sheds 11 times during its 13½-year career, ultimately being withdrawn from Patricroft in October 1966.
R. D. Stephens

Right:
How times have changed at Euston. This was the scene 39 years ago: English Electric Type 4 (Class 40) No D255 (later 40 055) arrives with an up express as No 73013 awaits its next duty. The '5MT' was then allocated to Bletchley; its career had begun at Millhouses in August 1951 and (after nine transfers) would end at Bolton in May 1966. *W. P. Power*

On the London Midland Region

Right:
In October 1964 a rake of brick empties passes through Fenny Stratford *en route* for Fletton Works at Millbrook, headed by Bletchley-allocated No 73013. *E. J. S. Gadsden*

Left:
No 73096 leaves Bredon with a Birmingham New Street–Worcester–Bristol stopping train on 22 April 1964. This station would close to passenger traffic on 4 January 1965. *D. Cross*

Right:
A busy scene at Bromsgrove station on 22 July 1961: Midland '4F' 0-6-0 No 44463 arrives with a Worcester Shrub Hill–Birmingham New Street local train as Canklow-allocated No 73002 passes with a southbound express. The following year the '5MT' would be transferred to the Southern Region, where it would remain until withdrawn in March 1967.
G. D. King

Below:
A fine winter shot of Gloucester Horton Road's No 73021 climbing the 1-in-37 Lickey Incline with a train of empty coal wagons on 28 December 1964. The absence of exhaust at the rear indicates there was a diesel banker. Following an initial two-year spell at Chester, No 73021 had become a Western Region engine and would end its days at Oxford, in August 1965. *F. A. Haynes*

Left:
The North Wales Coast main line was well used by the Standard '5MTs'. No 73043 enters Deganwy on the Llandudno branch during its time (October 1953 to May 1958) allocated to Patricroft. *K. Field*

Right:
It is hard to believe, but No 73035 is in green livery. A Patricroft engine at the time, it is shown passing Mollington, on one of the specials run to mark the end of the through Paddington–Birkenhead service on 4 March 1967. This locomotive had been new to Polmadie in August 1953 but stayed only one month before moving to Shrewsbury, where it spent most of its working life before being transferred to Patricroft and ultimately withdrawn in January 1968. *Gavin Morrison*

Left:
Patricroft's No 73073 passes Winwick Junction (just north of Warrington) at the head of the 10.38 Manchester Exchange–Bangor on 28 August 1965. New to Patricroft in December 1954, this locomotive was transferred frequently between sheds — including Bath Green Park, Leicester Midland, Millhouses, Holyhead, Llandudno Junction, Woodford Halse and Nuneaton — before returning in July 1965 to Patricroft, from where it would be withdrawn in November 1967. *Hugh Ballantyne*

Right:
No 73050 and No 73069, both by now based at Patricroft, leave Stalybridge on 27 April 1968 with one of the many steam specials run in the early months of that year; this one travelled via Huddersfield, Bradley Curve, the Calder Valley line and up over Copy Pit to Lancashire. Entering the station (in the background) is a trans-Pennine express is on its way to Liverpool. Following withdrawal in June 1968, No 73050 would subsequently be preserved; No 73069, surviving until the end of steam on British Rail in August 1968, would ultimately be less fortunate. *Gavin Morrison*

Below:
Another view of the special, crossing Ludgate Viaduct on the 1-in-65 gradient towards Copy Pit Summit. *Gavin Morrison*

Above:
Austerity 'WD' No 90671 of Oldham Lees shed shunts the yard at Diggle while Huddersfield Hillhouse-allocated No 73164 passes on a Leeds City–Manchester Exchange semi-fast, probably in the early 1960s. Diggle station and the entrance to Standedge Tunnel can just be seen in the background on the right. This location now has only two tracks, the yard area is full of trees, and the sidings behind the signalbox (which still exists) have become a car park.
J. Davenport

Left:
No 73039 going well over Saddleworth Viaduct, after almost 15 miles of climbing from Manchester Victoria, on 27 May 1967— only four months before withdrawal from Patricroft shed. The train is a relief to the morning Liverpool–Newcastle. The picture was taken from the platform of Saddleworth station, which would close to passengers on 7 October 1968.
Gavin Morrison

Left:
No 73096, displaying an untidy painted 9H shed code as applied to most of Patricroft's Standard '5MTs' before the end of steam, passes Comptons sidings, Wigan, with a coal train from Patricroft on 24 July 1967. Withdrawn four months later, this locomotive would eventually pass into preservation, running with a BR Type 1 tender in place of its original Type 1C. *J. H. Cooper-Smith*

Right:
A flower special from Chesterfield enters Southport Chapel Street station behind No 73074 on 24 August 1961, at which time the locomotive was allocated to Canklow. The London Street excursion platforms can be seen in the background. *R. S. Greenwood*

Right:
The Standard '5MTs' allocated to Patricroft were frequent performers on BR steam specials during the first half of 1968. This special is seen on 20 April 1968 at Rose Grove West, where the locomotives had stopped to take water, giving the passengers the opportunity to take photographs. Considerable effort has gone into cleaning No 73069, which is in unlined black livery and is being piloted by Caprotti No 73134. *Gavin Morrison*

Left:
A rather run-down No 73067 of Patricroft passes Shap Summit with a down freight on 16 December 1967, four months before it was withdrawn in March 1968. *Gavin Morrison*

Lower left:
The wide, open moorland countryside of the Settle–Carlisle line is the setting for this picture of No 73055 heading south between Ais Gill Summit and Shotlock Hill Tunnel at the head of an up relief on 3 June 1961. This locomotive had been new to Polmadie in June 1954 and would remain allocated there until withdrawn in May 1966. *Gavin Morrison*

Above:
Piloting an ex-LMS 'Jubilee', No 73142 heads a Manchester–St Pancras express past Chinley Junction, its 15C (Leicester Midland) shedplate dating the picture to between December 1956 (when the locomotive was new) and January 1959. Having spent most of its working life in the Leicester/Derby area, No 73142 would end its days at Patricroft, in April 1968. *N. Fields*

Above:
Green-liveried No 73031 pauses at Sheffield Midland with the 4.45pm from Bradford Forster Square to Bristol Temple Meads. The locomotive's 82B (Bristol St Philip's Marsh) shedplate suggests the picture was taken in the latter half of 1957. *T. G. Hepburn*

Right:
The first of the Caprotti Standard '5MTs', No 73125, makes an interesting picture running in undercoat on a trial run on the 2.50pm Manchester Central–Derby local train, seen near Breadsall crossing on 29 June 1956. *R. J. Buckley*

Above:
A picture of No 73031 fitted with air-brake equipment, which was removed after trials with air-braked freight trains. It is seen at Derby station with some empty stock on 16 September 1954. *P. H. Wells*

Below:
When only a few days old, an immaculate No 73004 carries out one of its first duties for Leicester Midland shed, being seen working a Leicester–Peterborough train on 15 June 1951. *P. H. Wells*

Right:
No 73073 of Leicester Midland shed (15C) makes a vigorous start from Stamford Town with a summer special on 1 June 1959. This locomotive had begun its career at Patricroft in December 1954 and, after eight transfers, would end its days back at the same shed, in November 1967. *P. H. Wells*

Left:
A very interesting picture of No 73001 piloting No 73000 at the head of a Derby Research Team special vacuum-fitted express coal train, with dynamometer car, near Harpenden Common at a controlled speed of 40mph on 26 October 1952. The train carries a Class C headlamp, being an express freight with not less than 50% of the wagons vacuum-braked and connected to the engines. These trial coal trains were probably the first ever to run under express-freight conditions. *E. D. Briton*

Right:
Leicester Midland's No 73003 is well cleaned as it heads past Hendon on 9 May 1953. It had been allocated to the shed from new in June 1951, staying until transfer in January 1958 to the Western Region, where it would remain until withdrawn from Oxford in June 1965. *A. R. Carpenter*

Left:
An early picture of brand-new
No 73000 at Neasden shed, taken
shortly before or after 26 April 1951,
when this locomotive went on display
at Marylebone station for inspection
by the Railway Executive. Between
November 1951 and March 1952
No 73000 was allocated to Stratford
and as such was the only Standard
'5MT' ever allocated to an ex-Great
Eastern shed. *C. C. B. Herbert*

On the Eastern and North Eastern Regions

Left:
In December 1956 and January 1957
Neasden shed received five brand-new
Standard '5MTs' — Nos 73155-9.
Their stay was brief, Nos 73155/6
lasting 1½ years, while the others had
gone by September 1957. It is thus
not surprising that pictures of them
working the main Great Central
expresses are somewhat rare;
this picture shows No 73157 in
immaculate condition at the head
of the down 'Master Cutler'
approaching Woodford Halse on
27 May 1957. *M. Mitchell*

Left:
While allocated to Woodford Halse,
No 73045 approaches Brackley at the
head of the 4.39pm Marylebone–
Nottingham Victoria on 9 May 1964.
New to Leeds Holbeck in November
1953, this locomotive moved to the
Great Central line at Leicester in
September 1959, staying at ex-GCR
sheds until transferred to Shrewsbury
in June 1964; it would end its days at
Patricroft, in August 1967.
M. Mensing

Right:
On 26 September 1964, during its time at Woodford Halse, No 73000 heads a Woodford Halse–Neasden coal train out of Princes Risborough. *Brian Stephenson*

Below:
A fine winter scene on the Great Central main line in January 1963, featuring ex-LMS Stanier '5MT' No 45277 (on the 12.25pm Nottingham Victoria–Marylebone) overtaking Standard '5MT' No 73066 on a coal train in Whetstone sidings. *C. P. Walker*

Left:
An undated picture of No 73162 passing Chaloners Whin Junction at the head of a Lowestoft–York express. The train is leaving a section of the East Coast main line which has since been closed and replaced by a more direct route; the lines on the right go to Sheffield and Leeds (and now also to King's Cross). *P. Ransome-Wallis*

Below:
No 73169 leaves Scarborough on the 4.19pm to Bradford, possibly in the first half of 1959, when this locomotive had a two-month spell allocated to Scarborough. It spent the first six years of its short (9½-year) career allocated to the York/Leeds/Wakefield area before being transferred to the Southern Region, from where it would be withdrawn in October 1966. *A. M. Ross*

Right:
Another undated picture, taken between August 1951 and September 1953, when No 73012 was allocated to Leeds Holbeck. The locomotive is seen leaving Bradford Forster Square with a train for Skipton.
E. Blakey

Right:
No 73000 hurries through the southern outskirts of Leeds at Stourton on a Bristol–Bradford Forster Square on 23 March 1961, when the locomotive was allocated to Canklow. The Freightliner terminal now occupies the right of this picture.
Gavin Morrison

Right:
Another view of a Bristol–Bradford Forster Square express passing Stourton, Leeds, this time headed by No 73031 — a Bristol Barrow Road locomotive in Brunswick green. It is seen passing ex-LMS '8F' 2-8-0 No 48126 on a down coal train.
Gavin Morrison

Left:
Huddersfield's Standard '5MT' No 73163 being prepared outside Leeds City station prior to piloting the 9.55am Newcastle–Liverpool Lime Street over the Pennines on 26 June 1960. *Gavin Morrison*

Right:
No 73163 makes a fine sight piloting rebuilt 'Royal Scot' No 46106 *Gordon Highlander* — unique among 'Royal Scots' in having straight smoke-deflectors — on the 9.55 Newcastle–Liverpool Lime Street on 26 June 1960. Allocated to Huddersfield Hillhouse shed for nearly six of its 7$\frac{3}{4}$ years of service, No 73163 would end its days at Patricroft, in November 1965. *Gavin Morrison*

Left:
Another Standard '5MT' on local service in West Yorkshire, this time Normanton's No 73167, seen heading west between Mirfield and Heaton Lodge Junction on 10 June 1960. *Gavin Morrison*

Right:
A picture taken from Springwood Junction signalbox (between the tunnels to the west of Huddersfield) showing one of Huddersfield Hillhouse's Standard '5MTs' — No 73164 — heading the 12.10pm local train to Manchester Exchange on 23 May 1959. *Gavin Morrison*

Below:
Patricroft's No 73039 climbs the steep bank on the Huddersfield line from Whitehall Junction, Leeds, with a Summer Saturday-only Newcastle–Llandudno train on 8 July 1967. Allocated to Patricroft, this locomotive would be withdrawn two months later. *Gavin Morrison*

Above:
Patricroft's Caprotti No 73134 pilots ex-LMS 'Jubilee' No 45613 *Kenya* over the Pennines on an evening Newcastle–Liverpool Lime Street express on 24 May 1960.

The train is seen just west of Gledholt Junction, Huddersfield, tackling the seven-mile climb (mainly at 1 in 105) from Huddersfield to Marsden. *Gavin Morrison*

Right:
No 73156 emerges from Bowling Tunnel near Bradford on the Summer Saturdays-only Bridlington–Bradford Exchange on 2 July 1966. Having begun its career working Great Central-line expresses from Neasden shed in December 1956, this locomotive would eventually become the 177th locomotive to be rescued from Barry Scrapyard, in October 1986, and is currently undergoing restoration on the Great Central Railway. *Gavin Morrison*

Left:
A fine picture of No 73106 crossing the Forth Bridge with an up express. The 63A (Perth) shedplate suggests that the photograph was taken between October 1957 and June 1964, when No 73106 moved to Corkerhill for its final year of service before withdrawal in June 1965.
E. R. Wethersett

Below:
Polmadie's No 73033 stands inside Edinburgh Princes Street station at the head of a stopping train, probably for Glasgow, when new in August 1953. The locomotive remained at Polmadie for only a month before being transferred to Shrewsbury; following numerous further reallocations, it would be withdrawn from Patricroft in January 1968. *Ian Allan Library*

Right:
A summer Glasgow–Morecambe relief heads through the Clyde Valley past Elvanfoot on 4 July 1964 behind Polmadie's No 73098 and Carlisle Kingmoor's Stanier Class 5MT No 44901. No 73098 would be withdrawn from Polmadie in March 1966; Elvanfoot station had an even shorter life expectancy, being closed to passengers from 4 January 1965.
D. Cross

Right:
Two empty-stock workings at the north end of Beattock yard on 11 July 1956. No 73062 of Motherwell stands alongside ex-LMS Class 5 No 45310 of Bushbury shed near Wolverhampton. The stock was being sent north for the Glasgow holidays; No 45310, with 20 coaches in tow, would definitely need assistance up Beattock Bank! Having spent nearly two years at Motherwell, No 73062 would move to Polmadie for the rest of its career, withdrawal coming in June 1965. *Gavin Morrison*

Right:
Aided by a banking engine (clearly visible in the background), Motherwell's No 73061 has 12 coaches in tow as it passes Greskine signalbox on Beattock Bank with a down express on 19 July 1959. This was another Standard '5MT' to spend all its days at Polmadie except for 20 months (1955-7) at Motherwell.
Gavin Morrison

Left:
Superpower for a Glasgow–Edinburgh Slateford freight on 13 August 1962. Standard '5MT' No 73063 of Polmadie pilots rebuilt 'Royal Scot' No 46107 *Argyll & Sutherland Highlander*, also from Polmadie, over the River Clyde near Uddingston. No 73063 would remain at Polmadie for its entire career, from September 1954 to June 1966. *N. Pollock*

Right:
The external condition of No 73122 — seen at the head of an empty coal train on 11 September 1959, when there were four main running lines through Dalry — suggests Glasgow's Corkerhill shed (67A) was short of cleaners. The locomotive would spend its entire career from January 1956 to September 1965 at Corkerhill.
Gavin Morrison

Left:
Perth's No 73005 climbs the 1-in-79 bank from Glasgow Buchanan Street past St Rollox shed (65B) to Robroyston, at the head of a morning express to Aberdeen in 1952.
Gavin Morrison

Above:
A clean No 73058 of Polmadie passes Cathcart North Junction on a local working, probably in the mid-1950s. The coloured background to the numberplate and shedplate — blue, red or green — was normal for locomotives in the Polmadie division at this time. *G. H. Robin*

Below:
On 21 April 1967 — a few weeks before the start of electric services — Polmadie's No 73079, in terrible external condition, heads the 17.03 Gourock–Glasgow Central near Bishopton. A lifelong Glasgow resident, this locomotive was new to Eastfield in May 1955 but stayed for just two months before moving to Corkerhill, where it remained for almost 12 years until transferred to Polmadie; it would be withdrawn the month after this photograph was taken. *W. A. C. Smith*

Left:
Nos 73077 and 73078 went new to Eastfield in May 1955 and seemed to spend most of their time on the West Highland line to Fort William. Here No 73078 pilots Stanier Class 5MT No 44956, also of Eastfield, past Craigendoran Junction with the 3.45pm from Glasgow Queen Street to Fort William on 11 August 1960. Its career would end in July 1966 at Carstairs shed, all but the last six months having been spent at Eastfield. *Gavin Morrison*

Below:
No 73077 waits at Arrochar & Tarbet for the 6.30am from Mallaig to Glasgow Queen Street, headed by Stanier Class 5MTs Nos 44973 and 44956, on 13 August 1960. No 73077 would spend 7½ years at Eastfield and then two at Corkerhill before withdrawal in January 1965. *Gavin Morrison*

Right:
Stormy conditions at Bridge of Orchy later the same day, as No 73077 and Class B1 4-6-0 No 61396 set off on the journey across Rannoch Moor with the 10.15am from Glasgow Queen Street to Mallaig.
Gavin Morrison

Below:
Another picture of No 73077, taken a year earlier as it pilots Stanier Class 5MT No 44956 near Ardlui on the overnight King's Cross–Fort William train during July 1959. *P. Ransome-Wallis*

Left:
With the help of a banker, No 73108 climbs the 1-in-41 Cowlairs Bank with the up 'Queen of Scots' on 13 July 1956. At this time Eastfield's Standard '5MTs' were often diagrammed for the up 'Queen of Scots' between Glasgow Queen Street and Edinburgh Waverley, where a Haymarket Pacific would take over for the run to Newcastle. No 73108 was new to Eastfield in December 1955, staying for just over 10 years before moving to Carstairs, from where it would be withdrawn in December 1966. *Gavin Morrison*

Left:
When only six months old, Eastfield's No 73108 makes an impressive sight as it passes Croy at the head of the 5.15pm Edinburgh Waverley–Glasgow Queen Street on 22 April 1956. Ten of this locomotive's 11 years of service would be spent working from Eastfield shed. *I. S. Pearsall*

Right:
A busy scene at the north end of Stirling station on the evening of 8 June 1957, featuring St Rollox's Caprotti Standard '5MT' No 73146 on a Glasgow Buchanan Street–Dundee train, Carlisle Kingmoor's ex-LMS Class 5MT No 45334 with a local service and Stirling-allocated Standard '4MT' 2-6-4T No 80125 in the bay platform. *Gavin Morrison*

Right:
By 1963 there was very little work for Perth's Stanier and Standard '5MTs', so, when the railbus normally used on the Crieff–Gleneagles service was unavailable, steam was substituted. This was the case on 11 May 1963, giving No 73007 one of its easiest duties during its career.
Gavin Morrison

Left:
No 73007 takes water at Gleneagles between duties on the Crieff local service on 11 May 1963. It was one of the five new to Perth in June/July 1951 and would stay until June 1964, eventually being withdrawn from Stirling in March 1966. The Crieff–Gleneagles service would finish on 6 July 1964. *Gavin Morrison*

Right:
When just a year old, No 73008 pauses at Forteviot with a stopping train for Perth on 22 July 1952. This locomotive went to the Rugby testing plant when new before entering service in April 1952 at Perth, and is seen in the fine condition typical of the shed's Standard '5MTs'. *Ian Allan Library*

Right:
The snow is still lying as No 73006 heads past Inchmagranachan with the 11.50am Perth–Inverness in the early 1950s. The photographer's Sunbeam Rapier car can be seen in the foreground. *W. J. V. Anderson*

Left:
The hard work is over for the firemen of Standard '5MT' No 73006 and Stanier No 44961 as they drift through Dalnaspidal station on the long descent to Killiecrankie (some 18 miles distant) on the morning train from Inverness to Glasgow Buchanan Street in April 1959. Dalnaspidal station would close to passenger traffic (such as it was) on 3 May 1965. No 73006 would spend 12½ years allocated to Perth before being transferred to Patricroft in July 1964 and ultimately withdrawn in March 1967. *Ian Allan Library*

Left:
Perth's No 73009 climbs through wild Scottish scenery near Dunphail on 13 May 1952. The 16-mile stretch of line from Forres to Dava, including gradients of between 1 in 70 and 1 in 60, would close in 1965. No 73009 would spend 11½ years allocated to Perth before moving to Corkerhill, from where it would be withdrawn in July 1966. *Ian Allan Library*

Class 4MT

Steam finished on the 'Cambrian Coast Express' on 4 March 1967. No 75033 was the locomotive in charge on the final day and was specially cleaned for the occasion and provided with headboard and an 89C (Machynlleth) shedplate, although actually allocated to Shrewsbury (89A). The locomotive made an excellent climb of the 1-in-52 gradient up Talerddig Bank and it is seen storming out of the cutting at the summit, after 14 miles of continuous climbing from Machynlleth. *Gavin Morrison*

Variations

Above and below:

Two pictures of the first Standard '4MT' 4-6-0, No 75000, when brand-new at Swindon in May 1951. It is attached to a BR Type 2 tender with capacity for 6 tons of coal and 3,500 gallons of water; the complete locomotive weighed 63 tons 6cwt empty and 67 tons 18cwt when full. The first 10 members of the class were allocated to the Western Region — mainly to Shrewsbury — and were fitted with coupling rods of a fluted design, as can be clearly seen here, but in due course these were mostly replaced with rods of rectangular section. *Ian Allan Library*

Above:
Nos 75065-79 were allocated to the Southern Region and because of the lack of water troughs were attached to Type 1B tenders with capacity for 7 tons of coal and 4,725 gallons of water. Nos 75065-9 went initially to Dover shed, and Nos 75070-9 to Exmouth Junction, where they stayed for a matter of a few months. This undated picture shows No 75069 whilst allocated to Eastleigh. *P. J. Sharpe*

Above:
In June 1957 No 75029 was fitted with double blastpipes and chimney at Swindon and emerged painted in BR lined green livery. The modification was a success but did little for the locomotive's appearance. It was decided to modify the whole class, but in fact only the Southern Region locomotives and six from the Western Region were done. No 75029 is seen ex works at Swindon during its time allocated to Oxford. *L. King*

Above:
The tall Swindon version of the double chimney remained a one-off, and Eastleigh Works produced its own, shorter, version, fitted to all the Southern Region locomotives and six Western Region engines. No 75078 (now preserved on the Keighley & Worth Valley Railway) shows off the variation at Basingstoke shed on 2 May 1962. *J. Scrace*

Below:
No 75029 eventually had its ugly Swindon double chimney replaced by the Eastleigh version. It is pictured in lined green at Eastleigh shed on 16 September 1961, whilst allocated to Tyseley in Birmingham. New to Plymouth Laira in May 1954, it would be transferred no fewer than 14 times before withdrawal from Stoke in August 1967 and purchase by artist David Shepherd. *Gavin Morrison*

Above:
No 75075 is piloting Standard '5MT' No 73043 out of Upwey South Tunnel on the 16.46 Weymouth–Waterloo extra on Easter Monday 1967. No 75075 was unique in being the only member of the class to be fitted with a Type BR1F tender, which held 5,625 gallons of water and 7 tons of coal and was originally attached either to a Standard '5MT' of the 73110-9 batch or to a '9F' 2-10-0. *J. H. Bird*

Left:
The last batch to be built at Swindon comprised Nos 75050-64, which emerged between November 1956 and July 1957 — 11 months after No 75079 had been completed; there should have been a further 10 for the Eastern Region, but this order was cancelled. Nos 75050-64 — all allocated to the London Midland Region — were attached to Type 2A tenders which externally were very similar to the Type 2, except they were fitted with a fall plate and gangway doors, as well as pick-up apparatus for use if required. No 75061 is seen at Derby on 27 April 1963.
R. A. Panting

Left:
The first '4MT' 4-6-0, No 75000, looking immaculate in BR lined green livery. The 82C shedplate suggests allocation to Swindon shed, where this picture was taken on 8 September 1957, but according to some records it was allocated to Shrewsbury at the time. It would survive until December 1965, having spent all its time based on the Western Region and ending up at Worcester. *Gavin Morrison*

On Shed

Below:
No 75067 with single chimney is pictured on the turntable at Ramsgate shed. This was the first of the class to be withdrawn — in October 1964, after just over nine years' service on the Southern Region. *J. Davenport*

Left:
Chester's No 75035 glistens in the evening sunshine at Llandudno Junction shed on 29 March 1959, together with unrebuilt 'Patriot' No 45546 *Fleetwood*, which can just be seen on the left. No 75035 began its career in August 1953 at Bletchley and moved around the London Midland Region until finishing its days in July 1967 as a Shap banker allocated to Tebay. *Gavin Morrison*

Right:
For many years the Somerset & Dorset line had double-chimney Nos 75071-3 allocated for working local trains. After the Western Region took over in 1958 it drafted in Standard '4MT' 4-6-0s *c*1961 to replace the ageing ex-LMS 4-4-0s used to pilot expresses over the Mendips. No 75002, in green livery and without shedplate, stands at Bath Green Park shed on 23 April 1962, having been reallocated to Templecombe in September 1961. It would eventually be withdrawn from Stoke shed in August 1967. *Gavin Morrison*

Right:
The Standard '4MT' 4-6-0s were seldom seen in the North East, but in February 1964 No 75046 of Liverpool Bank Hall was captured on Darlington shed following a visit to the adjacent works. It was one of the batch of five (Nos 75045-9) which went new to Accrington in October 1953 and which all moved to Bank Hall in November 1955, where most stayed for several years. No 75046 would end its days at Stoke in May 1967. *Gavin Morrison*

Right:
A picture of No 75034 taken on 30 June 1963 at its then home shed of Aston, Birmingham. During its 14½ years of service this locomotive wandered the London Midland Region, being reallocated no fewer than 16 times and ending up at Carnforth, from where it was withdrawn in February 1968. *A. W. Martin*

Left:
On 11 September 1960, during its 6½ years at Bath Green Park, No 75071 stands on shed between duties on the Somerset & Dorset line. *F. J. Saunders*

Left:
Now with double chimney and in terrible condition, No 75071 is seen during 1967 at Croes Newydd shed, Wrexham, where it had been allocated for nearly three years prior to its final transfer to Stoke. It would be withdrawn in August 1967.
A. O. Wynn

Right:
No 75027 was a long way from its then home shed of Liverpool Bank Hall when photographed on Eastleigh shed, waiting to be admitted to the works, on 19 April 1965. Having started its career at Plymouth Laira in May 1954, piloting expresses over the South Devon banks, it would become one of the last of its class to be withdrawn, in August 1968 from Carnforth shed, eventually passing into preservation on the Bluebell Railway. *Gavin Morrison*

Left:
A line-up outside Skipton shed on 20 August 1966 featuring No 75041 alongside Leeds Holbeck Stanier '8F' No 48157 and another Standard '4MT' 4-6-0. No 75041 spent two years at Skipton before moving to Carnforth when the shed closed, being withdrawn in January 1968. *Gavin Morrison*

Right:
In superb external condition and with white buffers, No 75007 stands at its home shed of Oxford on 3 June 1962. It appears to be in unlined green livery and is unusual in having a large emblem on the tender. It would eventually be withdrawn from Yeovil Town shed in March 1965 after just over 14 years' service. *M. York*

Above:
Seen at Crewe Works after an overhaul on 3 April 1966, No 75009 appears to be in unlined black livery, which may have made it unique within the class. A Llandudno Junction locomotive at the time, it had started life at Shrewsbury in October 1951 and was allocated to successive Western and London Midland Region sheds, eventually being withdrawn from Carnforth in June 1967. *G. M. Cox*

Below:
The first of three pictures of the Southern Region double-chimney locomotives. The modification improved the performance of these capable machines and they were popular amongst engineman on duties where the larger Class 5 was prohibited on account of axle load. No 75068 stands at its home shed of Eastleigh on 15 August 1961. *Gavin Morrison*

Above:
No 75074 had lost its front number and shedplate by the time it was photographed out of steam at Eastleigh on 2 October 1966. *Gavin Morrison*

Below:
The double-chimney Standard '4MT' 4-6-0s were well liked by the crews of Basingstoke shed, where many of these locomotives were allocated during their careers. No 75076 stands outside the shed on 24 September 1966 in front of a Bulleid Light Pacific. *Gavin Morrison*

Left:
In terrible external condition, No 75068 hurries a Plymouth–Brighton train near Angmering in March 1966. This was normally a 'West Country' / 'Battle of Britain' working or, failing that, a Standard '5MT'. *J. A. M. Vaughan*

On the Southern Region

Above:
Whilst allocated to Nine Elms, No 75077 passes through pleasant countryside between Deepdene and Betchworth at the head of the 11.05 Reading South–Redhill on 24 October 1964. *J. Scrace*

Above:
No 75075 near Basingstoke at the head of the 1.33pm to Waterloo on August Bank Holiday (4 August) 1958. The locomotive is in original condition with single chimney.
M. Mensing

Right:
No 75079 was the last of the Southern Region's Standard '4MTs' to receive a double chimney, in November 1961. The locomotive is pictured working an up semi-fast train between Swaythling and Eastleigh on 18 August 1961.
Gavin Morrison

Right:
On a very dull 31 May 1964 — the day Redbridge Viaduct was opened to traffic — No 75067 passes Chandlers Ford at the head of a diverted 11.20 Portsmouth–Bristol. This locomotive would be withdrawn five months later. *M. J. Fox*

Above:
Skipton-allocated No 75041 is a long way from home as it heads a local Southampton–Bournemouth train past the extensive roadworks for the new flyover at Totton, west of Southampton, on 9 September 1965. The locomotive was in the area because it had just been to Eastleigh Works for attention. It was new to Bedford in September 1953 and would survive almost to the end of steam, being withdrawn from Carnforth in January 1968. *Gavin Morrison*

Left:
No 75075 became unique among '4MT' 4-6-0s as the only one to acquire a BR1F tender, as seen in this picture of the locomotive taken between Brockenhurst and Sway on 10 September 1966. The BR1F tenders were attached to the Southern-allocated batch of BR Standard '5MTs' (Nos 73110-9), so presumably this example came from a withdrawn locomotive. No 75075 would survive until the end of steam on the Southern Region in July 1967. *M. Mensing*

Right:
No 75070 emerges from under the roof of Bournemouth Central station as it heads for the shed on 22 July 1966. This locomotive was new to Exmouth Junction in October 1955 and stayed on the Western section until January 1959, when it moved to Stewarts Lane. It moved back to the Western section at Nine Elms in August 1959 and would eventually be withdrawn from Eastleigh in September 1966. *Gavin Morrison*

Right:
The Bournemouth–Birkenhead express prepares to leave Bournemouth Central station on 9 June 1962, headed by Eastleigh-allocated No 75067. The following November it would be transferred to the Central section at Brighton but would return to Eastleigh in December 1963, staying until withdrawn in October 1964 — the first of its class to go, after just over nine years in service.
Gavin Morrison

Right:
On Sunday 4 June 1967 BRCW Type 3 (Class 33) diesel-electric No D6569 pilots No 75074 on an up freight approaching Dorchester West station. The '4MT' would be withdrawn just one month later.
M. Mensing

Left:
In June 1956 the Somerset & Dorset was allocated four Class 4MTs — Nos 75070-3. No 75070 was transferred away after nine months, but the other three remained for between eight and 9½ years, used primarily on local services and piloting duties. They were joined from February 1960 by additional members of the class, which arrived to take over the duties of the ex-LMS Class 2P 4-4-0s. Here green-liveried No 75023 (recently reallocated to Templecombe from Gloucester Barnwood) and unrebuilt 'West Country' No 34041 *Wilton* leave Bath with the 'Pines Express' on 9 September 1961; the '2Ps' had been used that morning to pilot northbound trains, before being placed in store for the final time. *Gavin Morrison*

Left:
Another view of No 75023, this time piloting Standard '5MT' No 73047 with the southbound 'Pines Express' on the 1-in-50 climb out of Bath towards Devonshire Tunnel. No 75023 would stay on the S&D for just one year before moving on, to Machynlleth, Croes Newydd and finally Stoke until withdrawal in January 1966. *Gavin Morrison*

Left:
The driver of No 75071 keeps a close eye ahead as he heads a train along the ex-Somerset & Dorset line on 27 July 1963 *Hugh Ballantyne*

Below:
With only another mile to go to the 811ft summit at Masbury, the southbound 'Pines Express', headed by No 75023 and unrebuilt 'West Country' No 34041 *Wilton*, is seen near Binegar on 9 September 1961. *Gavin Morrison*

Right:
No 75027 pilots Standard Class 5MT No 73054 as they tackle the almost continuous eight-mile climb, mainly 1 in 50, from Evercreech Junction to Masbury Summit on 12 August 1961. The train is a Summer Saturdays-only Bournemouth West–Derby and is approaching the twin-bore tunnels at Winsor Hill. *Gavin Morrison*

Left:
In the early 1960s there was probably no other line in the country that produced the varied permutations of motive power that could be observed on the S&D on summer Saturdays. In a combination of old and new, '4MT' 4-6-0 No 75009 pilots ex-LMS Class 4F 0-6-0 No 44417 near Wellow at the head of a Cleethorpes–Exmouth train on 28 July 1962. No 75009 would spend just over a year (between September 1961 and November 1962) allocated to Templecombe before moving on, ultimately finishing its career at Carnforth in August 1968. *Gavin Morrison*

Centre left:
No 75072 spent 9½ years working over the Somerset & Dorset line before being withdrawn from Templecombe in December 1965. On 28 July 1962 it was piloting a Standard '5MT' on a Bournemouth–Leeds express, pictured entering Wellow. *Gavin Morrison*

Lower left:
'4MT' No 75027 and 'West Country' No 34039 *Boscastle* pass Binegar, a mile short of Masbury Summit, at the head of a heavy 12-coach express for Bournemouth on 9 September 1961. Both locomotives are now preserved — No 75027 on the Bluebell Railway and No 34039 on the Great Central. *Gavin Morrison*

Above right:
No 75027 and unrebuilt 'West Country' No 34041 *Wilton* burst out of one of the single-bore tunnels at Chilcompton at the head of a heavy express for Bournemouth on 12 August 1961. The tunnels were situated about halfway up the steep (1-in-50) climb from Radstock to the summit at Masbury. *Gavin Morrison*

Right:
In terrible external condition, No 75072 leaves Evercreech Junction for Bath at the head of a stopping train on 1 January 1966. Operating the same day was one of a number of Somerset & Dorset farewell specials run in the early part of 1966, hence the crowd of photographers. *Gavin Morrison*

Left:
The signalbox has gone and there are more gorse bushes in the foreground (and there would certainly be more than two cars on the road), but otherwise the scene at Aller Junction, just west of Newton Abbot, has changed very little since this picture was taken in 1958. Looking rather grubby, Shrewsbury-allocated No 75000 pilots a clean ex-GWR 'Castle' — No 5058 *Earl of Clancarty* — on a Penzance–Paddington express. The 'Castle' would put in 26 years of service but No 75000 would manage only 14½, being withdrawn from Worcester in December 1965.
Ian Allan Library

On the Western Region

Right:
It looks as if 21 August 1954 was a dull day at Newton Abbot. The BR Standard combination of Swindon's '4MT' No 75001 and 'Britannia' No 70018 *Flying Dutchman* head out of the station and prepare to tackle Dainton Bank with the 11am Paddington–Penzance. The '4MT' would be withdrawn from Yeovil Town in December 1964. *T. E. Williams*

Left:
Five Class 4MTs — Nos 75025-9 — went new to Plymouth Laira (83D) in April and May 1954. Nos 75027 and 75029 stayed only three months but the others remained for two years, being used for piloting trains over the South Devon banks and on other secondary workings. No 75028 heads a six-coach Liverpool–Penzance working past Stoneycombe Quarry in 1954. *Ian Allan Library*

Right:
When only a month old, an immaculate No 75004, allocated to Bristol Bath Road (82A), heads a semi-fast from Swindon to Paddington into Sonning Cutting on 1 September 1951. During its 15½ years this locomotive would move nine times, mainly within the Western Region, before ending its days at Shrewsbury, in March 1967. *K. W. Wightman*

Below:
A well-timed shot of 'WD' 2-8-0 No 90630 and '4MT' No 75003 passing at Haddenham on the ex-Great Western/Great Central joint line north of Princes Risborough. No 75003, in lined green, was one of the seven WR-allocated '4MTs' to receive a double chimney. The picture is undated but is certainly post-1959. *M. J. Esau*

Left:
No 75029 was the first '4MT' to be modified, when, in June 1957, following draughting tests, it was fitted with a double blastpipe and chimney at Swindon. Soon after modification, on 23 September 1957, when allocated to Oxford, the locomotive is seen tackling the 1-in-100 gradient from Honeybourne to Chipping Campden with the 1.40pm Hereford–Oxford.
As is apparent from the picture, the chimney itself was less than elegant, but the basic modification was a success, and the intention was to modify the whole class. However, with impending dieselisation, only the Southern Region locomotives and six more for the Western Region would be done, at Eastleigh, which thankfully altered the chimney design. *M. Mensing*

Centre left:
No 75026 spent its first two years (1954-6) allocated to Plymouth Laira, piloting 'Kings', 'Castles' and others over the South Devon banks. When photographed at Birmingham Snow Hill on 2 May 1959, by which time it had moved to Tyseley, it was once again piloting a 'King', having been attached at Leamington to help No 6008 *King James II* deal with the climb into Snow Hill station following a temporary 5mph restriction just outside Snow Hill Tunnel. *M. Mensing*

Lower left:
The empty stock for the 5.45pm to Stratford and Worcester pulls into Birmingham Snow Hill on 9 July 1960 behind No 75025 of Worcester shed (85A). Although transferred to other sheds in the intervening period, this locomotive would return to Worcester prior to withdrawal in December 1965. *M. Mensing*

Left:
One of the '4MTs' to receive a double chimney, No 75006 restarts the 17.35 Birmingham Snow Hill–Lapworth from Knowle & Dorridge station on 19 August 1965. The painted 5D shed code denotes allocation to Stoke, from where the locomotive would be withdrawn two years later. *M. Mensing*

Right:
A powerful picture of No 75027 in the Birmingham suburbs as it heads a down fitted freight from Morris Cowley in the late evening light at Widney Manor on 8 July 1958. This locomotive would survive to the end of BR steam, being withdrawn from Carnforth in August 1968 and then passing into preservation. It can now be seen on the Bluebell Railway. *M. Mensing*

Left:
Another picture of No 75006 in charge of the 17.35 Birmingham Snow Hill–Lapworth, this time approaching Widney Manor station on 20 September 1965. *M. Mensing*

Left:
Only just on the Western Region, Derby-allocated No 75060 passes Norton Junction, just south of Worcester, with the 2.44pm Worcester Shrub Hill–Gloucester on 24 August 1963. From this point the WR line continued to Evesham, but the train is on the spur to Abbotswood Junction, where it will enter the London Midland Region. *M. Mensing*

Left:
No 75025 crosses Malvern Common with the 5.40pm Birmingham Snow Hill–Kidderminster– Malvern Wells on 3 May 1958. The wooden fence in the background indicates the location of the erstwhile line to Upton-upon-Severn. At the time of the photograph No 75025 was allocated to Worcester, where it would be allocated three times, the last ending with withdrawal in December 1965. *M. Mensing*

Left:
No 75021 was new to Cardiff Canton in November 1953 and would stay for nearly five years. On Easter Monday (7 April) 1958 it is seen working the 9.45am Birmingham Snow Hill– Cardiff express past Tram Inn station, which would lose its passenger service barely two months later, on 9 June. No 75021's working life would be spent mainly on the Western Region but would draw to a close at Carnforth, in February 1968. *M. Mensing*

Above:

The Cambrian lines were part of the Western Region until September 1963, when they passed to the London Midland Region. The LMR was quick to replace the ex-Great Western motive power — especially the 'Manor' class, which had been associated with the lines for many years — with BR Standards, mainly '4MT' 4-6-0s. However, '4MTs' were working the Cambrian lines long before the LMR took over, No 75020 having been allocated to Machynlleth as early as June 1959. Here No 75002 pilots an ex-GWR '43xx' class 2-6-0 on the approach to Llandanwg with a through train from Paddington to Pwllheli one Saturday in June 1959, although this particular example would not be transferred to the Cambrian lines until September 1962. *G. F. Bannister*

On Cambrian Lines

Right:

Aberystwyth shed kept its Great Western 'Manors' in spotless condition for working the 'Cambrian Coast Express', but unfortunately this care was never lavished upon the Standard '4MTs'. On 2 June 1962 the down train, complete with headboard, leaves Welshpool behind a dirty Machynlleth-allocated No 75021, piloting No 7823 *Hook Norton Manor*. No 75021 would survive almost to the end of steam, putting in 14 years and four months' work and thus slightly bettering No 7823's 13 years and eight months. *Gavin Morrison*

Above:
Buttington Junction, three miles north of Welshpool, was the point where the line to Shrewsbury (ex-LNWR/GWR) left the Cambrian main line.
On 5 March 1956 No 75005 of Oswestry shed makes ready to depart as an ex-GWR 0-6-0 arrives.
Hugh Ballantyne

Left:
In the first of a sequence of four pictures taken on 11 February 1967, No 75048 prepares to leave Aberystwyth station with 'Cambrian Coast Express' to Paddington, which it would work as far as Shrewsbury. The locomotive has been well cleaned by enthusiasts and displays the old WR 89C shedplate for Machynlleth, in place of the LMR's 6F.
Gavin Morrison

Right:
Only 4½ miles into its journey, No 75048 passes Bow Street station, one of the passing-points on the first section to Machynlleth.
Gavin Morrison

Right:
Having climbed steadily for the last 10 miles from Machynlleth No 75048 starts the really steep ascent at 1 in 52 for the final four miles to Talerdigg Summit as it passes Llanbrynmair.
Gavin Morrison

Left:
No 75048 arrives at Welshpool station, 61 miles from Aberystwyth. The train will leave the ex-Cambrian main line at Buttington for the last 17 miles to Shrewsbury, which will involve a further five miles of climbing at between 1 in 80 and 1 in 100. The station has now moved to a new site in Welshpool.
Gavin Morrison

Right:
The last steam-hauled 'Cambrian Coast Express' ran on 4 March 1967, No 75033 of Croes Newydd hauling the last up working. A lot of effort was put in the night before to make the locomotive presentable for the occasion, and a fine job was done, No 75033 receiving a home-made numberplate, an 89C shedplate and a fine 'Cambrian Coast Express' headboard. Looking superb, it is shown ready to depart Aberystwyth for Shrewsbury. *Gavin Morrison*

Left:
No 75033 is now well into its stride as it passes Bow Street, at the foot of the 1-in-75 gradients either side of the station, and heads for Machynlleth. *Gavin Morrison*

Left:
The enthusiasts in the first two coaches are enjoying No 75033's progress up the climb from Machynlleth to Llanbrynmair, before the 1-in-52 slog to Talerdigg. The train is passing Cemmes Road, six miles from Machynlleth. *Gavin Morrison*

Above:
With not a trace of steam leaking from anywhere it shouldn't, No 75033 blasts through the cutting at Commins Coch, 1½ miles west of Cemmes Road. *Gavin Morrison*

Above:
Having climbed for 10 miles, No 75033 takes full advantage of the few yards of level track at Llanbrynmair before tackling the last 3½ miles at 1 in 52 to Talerddig Summit. The sight and sound were memorable, and the performance was a fitting one for the last steam-hauled up 'Cambrian Coast Express'. *Gavin Morrison*

Right:
Unfortunately no effort was made to clean the locomotive for the last down train, Shrewsbury shed providing a filthy green-liveried No 75006. The train is seen leaving Shrewsbury station. *Gavin Morrison*

Left:

No fewer than 45 of the 80 Standard Class 4MT 4-6-0s were allocated from new to the London Midland Region, where the type would be represented until the end of BR steam. Bletchley shed received a batch of 10 new examples (Nos 75030-9) in mid-1953 for working fast and stopping trains into Euston — duties they shared with BR Standard '4MT' (80xxx) 2-6-4Ts. This fine picture shows an immaculate No 75034 leaving Bletchley with a stopping train for Oxford when just over a year old, in September 1954. Nos 75030-5 moved on after around 18 months, mainly to the North Wales route; No 75034 would be transferred no fewer than 15 times before withdrawal from Carnforth in February 1968. *P. Ransome-Wallis*

Above:
Another picture taken at Bletchley, this time of No 75031 leaving on an up stopping train on the main line *c*1954.

Having been reallocated 13 times, mainly around North Wales, this locomotive would end its career at Stoke shed in February 1966. *P. Ransome-Wallis*

Left:
In steam days Birmingham New Street could always be relied upon to produce wonderfully atmospheric pictures. With steam everywhere, No 75021 prepares to leave with the 6.12am Derby– Bristol, whilst to the left is Ivatt '4MT' 2-6-0 No 43012 on the 8.27 to Ashchurch via Redditch. A Bristol Barrow Road locomotive when this photograph was taken in the late 1950s, No 75021 would last almost to the end of BR steam at Carnforth. *M. Mensing*

Right:
On 31 August 1957 the 9.20am Filey Holiday Camp–King's Norton leaves Birmingham New Street behind Leicester's No 75059. Like many other members of its class, this locomotive would end its days at Carnforth, in July 1967. *M. Mensing*

Left:
The 8am Newcastle Central–Cardiff General express enters Birmingham New Street's Platform 10 on 27 August 1960 behind No 75009 of Gloucester (Barnwood) and a very dirty Standard '5MT', No 73016. No 75009 would have a short spell on the Somerset & Dorset (see page 82) and, after many moves, end its days at Carnforth, being one of the last five to be withdrawn at the end of BR steam. *M. Mensing*

Left:
Another picture of No 75009 during its time at Gloucester Barnwood shed (August 1958 to September 1961). The locomotive is seen in 1959 heading a Gloucester–Bristol stopping train away from Yate station, which would close to passengers from 4 January 1965. *Ian Allan Library*

Above:
No 75002 pulls away from Ashchurch station at the head of the 2.40pm Worcester Shrub Hill– Bristol Temple Meads stopping train on 29 July 1961, at which time it was a Gloucester Barnwood locomotive. It would subsequently spend nine months on the Somerset & Dorset and after several moves finished its time at Stoke, in August 1967. *M. Mensing*

Right:
The telegraph wires — less of a problem for today's photographer — fail to detract from this picture of No 75013 on a local stopping train from Coventry to Nuneaton, taken near Bedworth on 19 November 1964. Visible in the background is Longford power station. Allocated to Bletchley at the time, the locomotive would survive until August 1967, ending its days at Stoke. *M. Mensing*

Left:
On a very wet 15 August 1963 No 75055 crosses Chinley Viaduct as it approaches Chinley South Junction with a local Manchester Central–Derby train. Curving away to the right is the Hope Valley line. A Derby locomotive at the time, No 75055 would end its days at Stoke, in May 1967. *G. T. Robinson*

Right:
An undated picture (probably taken in the late 1950s) showing No 75016 piloting ex-LMS 'Crab' 2-6-0 No 42871 on a Failsworth–Blackpool excursion at Heyside, between Oldham and Shaw. Unusually for a '4MT', No 75016 would be withdrawn from Colwick shed in June 1967, by which time this shed had been transferred to the London Midland Region. *J. Davenport*

Above:
A fine picture which captures well the scenery around Wigan, showing a slag heap, big Lancashire mill and church. The location is ¼ mile east of Pemberton station. Seen at the head of a local service on 13 June 1965,

No 75046 carries an 8K shedplate, reflecting the new code for Bank Hall shed, Liverpool, introduced in September 1963. After spending 11 years at Bank Hall, the locomotive would end its career at Stoke, in August 1967. *M. Mensing*

Left:
In April 1964 No 75032, then allocated to Liverpool Bank Hall, hurries a Blackpool–Liverpool train past Treales, near Kirkham. The locomotive would finish its days as a Shap banker, being withdrawn from Carnforth in February 1968. *J. Davenport*

Right:
A picture of another Bank Hall locomotive, No 75045, taken on 24 September 1960 and showing the earlier 27A shedplate. The train is a Bradford Exchange–Liverpool Exchange express, seen near Charlstown, between Hebden Bridge and Todmorden. No 75045 would be allocated to only three sheds during its career, spending its first two years at Accrington, then over 12 years at Bank Hall and a final three at Nuneaton before being withdrawn in April 1966. *Gavin Morrison*

Below:
During its second spell at Bank Hall, lasting from 1956 until withdrawal in 1966, No 75049 heads a Leeds Central–Liverpool Exchange express over the Rochdale Canal by means of Gauxholme Viaduct (between Todmorden and Walsden). *Gavin Morrison*

Left:
The '4MT' class was well represented on the North Wales lines, where the type basically replaced the Midland Compounds (and would in turn be replaced by BR Standard '5MTs'). On 8 April 1958 No 75010 leaves Llandudno Junction with an express for Chester. The locomotive would spend much of its career in North Wales but would end its days at Carnforth, in June 1967.
Gavin Morrison

Right:
No 75006, fitted with a double chimney in December 1960, prepares to leave Chester General station with the 17.55 to Barmouth on 30 May 1964. Its 6C shedplate denotes allocation to Croes Newydd, which had been transferred from the Western to the London Midland Region in September 1963. This locomotive would be withdrawn from Stoke in August 1967, having been reallocated many times during its 16 years of service. *J. S. Whiteley*

Left:
The 5.00pm Denbigh–Chester General arrives at Mold station on the last day of service — 28 April 1962 — headed by No 75033, then of Rhyl shed. This locomotive would be reallocated no fewer than 21 times during its career of just over 14 years, finally being withdrawn from Carnforth in April 1967. *M. Mensing*

Right:
The line between Lancaster Green Ayre and Morecambe closed on 3 January 1966. On 9 October 1965 No 75015 of Skipton was photographed underneath the electrification wires, approaching Scale Hall at the head of a local train. Following the closure of Skipton shed this locomotive would move to Carnforth, surviving until December 1967. *Gavin Morrison*

Above:
An unidentified Standard '4MT' climbs towards Blea Moor on a down freight as a rare gap opens in the clouds on 4 February 1967. *J. Goss*

Right:
Already pictured on pages 88, 89 and 95, No 75021 had only another eight months' service left when photographed at the head of an up ballast train leaving the Wennington line at Settle Junction on 13 June 1967. The end would come at Carnforth in February 1968.
Gavin Morrison

Left:
During its seven months allocated to Tebay, No 75032 gives Stanier Class 5MT No 45444 a helping hand on the climb to Shap at the head of the 10.45 Blackpool–Dundee on 22 July 1967. Upon Tebay's closure at the end of 1967, No 75032 would move to Carnforth but would survive there only until February 1968. *J. H. Cooper-Smith*

Left:
No 75024 banks a down freight (headed by Stanier Class 5MT No 45295) away from Tebay during its brief (five-month) spell as a Shap banker. It would be withdrawn from Tebay in December 1967. *L. A. Nixon*

Left:
A fine, atmospheric picture of an unidentified Standard '4MT' recovering at Grayrigg Summit after banking a train up the climb from Oxenholme on 21 July 1967. *J. H. Cooper-Smith*

Right:
The Grassington & Threshfield branch carried on to the end of BR steam. Standard Class 4MTs replaced the Midland '4F' 0-6-0s which had operated it for many years, and Skipton and (later) Carnforth sheds received many examples of the class for working out their final days on this duty. Here No 75021, devoid of numberplate, tackles the grade out of Skipton with some empty wagons for Swinden Quarry on 21 June 1967. It would be withdrawn eight months later. *Gavin Morrison*

Left:
Not long after being allocated to Carnforth in June 1967, double-chimney No 75020 appeared on the Grassington branch. It is seen climbing out of Skipton towards the former Embsay Junction, having just crossed over the Midland main line and A65 road, on 13 June 1967. This locomotive would survive until the end of steam operation in August 1968. *Gavin Morrison*

Right:
No 75026 spent only five months at Skipton before being transferred away to Tebay, ending its days on banking duties over Shap. During its stay at Skipton it frequently worked the Grassington branch and is shown on 17 March 1967 passing under the Skipton–Grassington road with some loaded wagons for the terminus. *Gavin Morrison*

Left:
End of the line at Grassington. An apparently run-down No 75042 prepares to leave the overgrown terminus with the daily pick-up freight back to Skipton on 6 October 1965. With the closure of Skipton shed the engine would move to Carnforth, surviving there until December 1967. *Gavin Morrison*

Above:
Nine months later, traffic at Grassington had dwindled to one wagon and a brake van, and the weeds had virtually obliterated the track. The station sign still survived, despite passenger services having ceased on 22 September 1930!

No 75015 prepares to leave for Skipton on 29 June 1966. The section between Swinden Quarry (now the terminus) and Grassington would close completely on 9 August 1969. The site is now a housing estate. *Gavin Morrison*

Right:
On 31 May 1968 British Rail operated the last steam-hauled freight over the Settle & Carlisle, from Rylston to Appleby. No 75019 was the chosen locomotive and is seen in the yard at Skipton prior to departure as the crew discuss the trip. No 75019 would get cleaner and cleaner as the end of steam approached, receiving attention on an almost daily basis from enthusiasts. *Gavin Morrison*

Below:
No 75019 crosses over the A65 road on the viaduct just north of Settle station as some locals go about their business, unaware of the significance of the passing train. *Gavin Morrison*

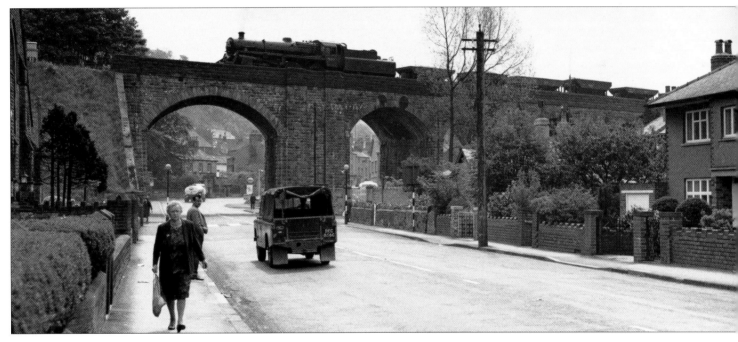

Right:
The crew entered into the spirit of the event and put up an excellent exhaust on the approach to Ribblehead station. The lines on the right lead into Ribblehead Quarry. *Gavin Morrison*

Left:
Having worked the last steam-hauled freight over the Settle–Carlisle the day before, No 75019 was back on its usual duty shunting wagons at Swinden Quarry on 1 June 1968. This location has since changed out of all recognition. *Gavin Morrison*

Left:
On 28 July 1968 — two weeks before the official end of steam on BR — Nos 75019 and 75027 storm south past Hellifield at the head of a special which they would work as far as Skipton, steam having been banned from the North Eastern Region by this time. This was probably the last working for these locomotives; No 75027 would ultimately pass into preservation, but No 75019 would not be so lucky. *Gavin Morrison*

Right:
During the last week of regular steam on BR, No 75048 pulls away from Silverdale 'box after a signal check on the Ulverston–Carnforth pick-up freight. The locomotive would be withdrawn on arrival at Carnforth. *K. P. Lawrence*

Right:

No Class 4MT was ever allocated to either the Eastern or the North Eastern Region, although until the early 1960s the locomotives (Nos 75015-9) new to Southport in 1952 were regular performers on locals via the Calder Valley main line to Bradford Exchange and Leeds Central. In addition, the batch (75045-9) new to Accrington in 1953 were often seen for a short time and occasionally appeared on Bradford/Leeds–Liverpool trains while allocated to Liverpool Bank Hall shed. Visits to Leeds City were unusual, though two pictures are included here, the first showing Nottingham-allocated No 75062 leaving with a local for Sheffield on 28 May 1960.
Gavin Morrison

On the Eastern and North Eastern Regions

Right:

The second view at Leeds City depicts No 75003 passing through the west end of the station with a local freight. Unfortunately there are no details for this rare working, although the locomotive's 84G (Shrewsbury) shedplate dates the picture to between August 1951 and December 1953. No 75003 would eventually become one of the minority to receive a double chimney. *K. Field*

Above:
Probably the only occasion in BR days on which a '4MT' 4-6-0 was coupled to an 'A4' Pacific. This unusual working occurred on 27 April 1966, when No 75019 was diagrammed to haul No 60010 *Dominion of Canada* from Leeds to Crewe Works to be prepared for export to Montreal in Canada.; the 'A4' had been sent to Darlington Works for a repair in May 1965 but was condemned instead, being sent to Darlington Bank Top shed, where it remained until 1966. The combination is seen leaving Neville Hill yard, with the shed's coaling plant visible behind the brake van. *Gavin Morrison*

Centre left:
Leicester-allocated No 75043 leaves Peterborough East — one of the few locations where '4MTs' ventured onto Eastern Region territory — on a local train for Leicester in September 1960. This locomotive would put in just over 14 years' service before being withdrawn from Carnforth in December 1967. *J. C. Baker*

Left:
In the late 1950s the 4.37pm Manchester Victoria Bradford Exchange was a regular working into North Eastern territory for the five Southport-allocated '4MTs' (Nos 75015-9). No 75017 is shown picking up water on Luddendenfoot troughs, just west of Sowerby Bridge on the Calder Valley line, on 25 July 1956. *Gavin Morrison*

In Preservation

Ex-Southern Region Standard '4MT' No 75078 was the 21st locomotive to be rescued from Barry, being saved by members of the Keighley & Worth Valley Railway in June 1972. Back in traffic by early 1977, it has worked on the K&WVR ever since but has never ventured onto the main line. It is seen approaching Damens Halt on 11 September 1977. *Gavin Morrison*

Above:
Double-chimney No 75069 was the 37th locomotive to leave Barry scrapyard, in March 1973, when it departed for the Severn Valley Railway. Its first main-line outing was on 2 March 1985, when it was photographed just east of Newport in South Wales. It subsequently operated several specials in the Midlands and on the Southern Region.
Gavin Morrison

Left:
No 75069 has been based at the Severn Valley Railway since entering preservation. It is seen approaching Foley Park Tunnel with a train for Kidderminster on 14 October 1989.
Gavin Morrison

Right:
Standard '4MT' No 75014 is probably the most widely travelled of the preserved Standard '4MT' and '5MT' locomotives. It was the 121st locomotive to leave Barry scrapyard, in February 1981; just over 14 years later, on 3 March 1995, it was out on its main-line test run from Derby to Sheffield and return, being seen passing Barrow Hill with the 10-coach test train. *Gavin Morrison*

Below:
Standard '5MT' No 73096 is, at the time of writing, the only member of the class available for use on the main line. It is seen here passing Edenbridge on 17 July 1999 en route for Canterbury at the head of the 'Canterbury Belle'. Based on the Mid-Hants Railway No 73096 can often be seen running over former Southern metals. *Rodney Lissenden*

Saved following the end of steam by artist David Shepherd, No 75029 went initially to the Longmoor Military Railway, before moving to Cranmore. It attended the Stockton & Darlington 150 celebrations and is pictured on 21 August 1975 with other locomotives at the exhibition which was staged in the bay platforms at the north end of Darlington station. *Gavin Morrison*

Above:
At the end of steam No 73050 was purchased from BR for preservation and for several years was visible from the East Coast main line, being parked in a siding just north of Peterborough station. The locomotive was destined for the Nene Valley Railway, where it has remained ever since.

Painted in BR Brunswick green, it has been named *City of Peterborough* but will always be associated with the Somerset & Dorset line, on which it spent many years working the main passenger services. It is seen on 20 April 1984 at Wansford. *Gavin Morrison*